6-14

EDGE BOOKS

HAUNTED AMERICA

BACHELOR'S GROVE CEMETERY

AND OTHER HAUNTINGS OF THE MIDWEST

by Matt Chandler

CAPSTONE PRESS
a capstone imprint

Edge Books are published by Capstone Press,
1710 Roe Crest Drive, North Mankato, Minnesota 56003
www.capstonepub.com

Library of Congress Cataloging-in-Publication Data
Cataloging-in-publication information is on file with the Library of Congress.
ISBN 978-1-4765-3913-3 (library binding)
ISBN 978-1-4765-5961-2 (eBook PDF)

Editorial Credits
Anthony Wacholtz, editor; Heidi Thompson, designer; Marcie Spence,
media researcher; Danielle Ceminsky, production specialist

Photo Credits
Benjamin Jeffries: 17, 18-19; Capstone: 5 (bottom); Cleveland Public Library
Photograph Collection, 5 (top); Corbis: Bettmann, 11; Getty Images: American Stock,
10, Richard Drew, 8; Grand Opera House, 14, 15; Newscom: University of Wisconsin-
Superior KRT, 26, 26-27; Shutterstock: John Brueske, 24-25, Triff, cover, 1; Tyler
Bennett, 21; Wikipedia: Magnus Mankse, 9, Matt Hucke, 7, 13, Mikefall2, 23

Direct Quotations
Page 6: Brad Steiger. "Real Ghosts, Restless Spirits and Haunted Places." Detroit,
Visible Ink Press, 2003, 355.
Page 13: "Lemp Stories." http://www.lempstories.com/textstories.htm
Page 23: "Ashmore—the Truth." http://blogs.wthitv.com/2010/10/29/ashmore-
the-truth/

Printed in the United States of America in Stevens Point, Wisconsin.
092013   007768WZS14

TABLE OF CONTENTS

From hotels to restaurants, the midwestern United States is filled with haunted places. People have reported thousands of spooky encounters with the dead. Are there logical explanations for these sightings? Or is the heartland of America home to some of the scariest ghosts in the world? Dare to read on and decide for yourself!

FRANKLIN CASTLE

The sight of the Franklin Castle can send shivers down anyone's spine. The 28-room stone castle has a **Gothic** look. According to legend, many murders and deaths have happened at the castle over the last 100 years.

Some people think the castle is haunted by those who died there. A young girl was killed in a secret passageway. Another girl was murdered in her bed. Owners of the home once found a collection of baby skeletons hidden in a secret room. Visitors and past owners have reported hearing crying babies when none were present.

The original owner of the castle was a man named Hannes Tiedemann. He supposedly murdered a woman in the castle. Many people have reported seeing "the woman in black." She is an **apparition** that sits in the tower of the castle looking out the window.

CITY: Cleveland, Ohio

FIRST REPORTED HAUNTING: 1930s

TYPES OF ACTIVITY: a baby crying, the ghost of a woman in black, doors exploding from the hinges

SCARY RANKING: 3

ACCESS: The castle is privately owned; tours are not available.

Hannes Tiedemann (left) with his wife, Louise, and their son, August

Gothic—in the style of art or architecture used in western Europe between the 1100s and 1500s
apparition—the visible appearance of a ghost

BACHELOR'S GROVE CEMETERY

There are few places more creepy than a cemetery after dark. Bachelor's Grove Cemetery in the Bremen Township in Illinois is no exception. It is considered to be one of the most haunted cemeteries in the United States. The last body was buried in Bachelor's Grove in 1989, but the cemetery gets plenty of visitors. There have been more than 100 reported **paranormal** events on the grounds since 1864.

Ghostly tales from Bachelor's include apparitions that have been seen wandering the graveyard. People have claimed to see the ghost of a woman carrying a baby. The woman wanders throughout the cemetery without a particular direction. When people approach her, she disappears.

CITY: Bremen, Illinois

FIRST REPORTED HAUNTING: 1860s

TYPES OF ACTIVITY: ghostly apparitions, unexplained glowing balls of light

SCARY RANKING: 4

ACCESS: The cemetery is open to the public.

"As I looked up, I saw the deceased woman's husband standing there ... I looked back down in the open grave and then looked back up and they were gone."

—a gravedigger at Bachelor's Grove Cemetery

paranormal—having to do with an unexplained event

The most famous ghost of Bachelor's Grove was first seen in the 1970s by two park rangers. They spotted a ghostly figure of a horse emerging from a pond outside the cemetery. The horse was pulling a plow with the ghost of an old man steering it. Legend says that in the 1800s, a farmer drowned in the pond when his horse dragged him in. The pond is also said to hold the bodies of people murdered during the **Prohibition.**

Another ghostly tale from Bachelor's involves a spooky creature. There is a story of a two-headed monster that has been seen running through the cemetery. There have even been paranormal events reported outside the cemetery. People have reported phantom cars on the nearby road that suddenly disappear.

Some people think that the hauntings in Bachelor's Grove Cemetery became more frequent after the rise of **vandalism** in the 1960s. Vandals knocked over tombstones and covered them in spray paint. Some vandals even broke into the graves and stole the bodies. Bones of the dead were found scattered across the cemetery.

the pond at Bachelor's Grove Cemetery

Prohibition—a time between 1920 and 1933 when it was illegal to make or sell alcohol in the United States

vandalism—the wrecking of property

BIOGRAPH THEATRE

John Dillinger was a bank robber in the early 1930s. He murdered at least 10 people during his crime spree. The Federal Bureau of Investigation (FBI) searched for Dillinger in 1934. FBI agents eventually tracked him down in Chicago, Illinois, on July 22, 1934. They approached him as he was leaving the Biograph Theatre. When confronted, he ran toward an alley. The agents shot and killed him.

Hauntings have been reported in the 80 years since Dillinger was killed. A ghost of a man matching the gangster's description has been seen outside the theater. Some witnesses have seen him in the alley, running away from the Biograph. The figure then collapses, just as Dillinger did the night he was shot by the FBI. Other visitors report cold spots and odd temperature changes inside the theater. Many have said they feel an unexplained sense of fear when walking past the alley.

CITY: Chicago, Illinois

FIRST REPORTED HAUNTING: 1940s

TYPES OF ACTIVITY: the ghost of gangster John Dillinger

SCARY RANKING: 2

ACCESS: The theatre is open to the public.

John Dillinger

People crowded around the front of the Biograph Theatre after John Dillinger was shot in 1934.

LEMP MANSION

The Lemp family earned a fortune brewing beer, but the family suffered several tragedies. The family **patriarch**, William Lemp, fatally shot himself in his bedroom in the mansion in 1904. Eighteen years later, his son William Jr. carried out the same act in the office. His sister Elsa and brother Charles followed the same fate.

The mansion was sold, and it was turned into a boarding house and eventually a restaurant. During construction, workers reported terrifying paranormal events. Doors slammed with no explanation. The workers often had tools disappear. They also described feeling like they were being watched. Some refused to finish the work. They were too scared to return to Lemp Mansion.

Eventually the work was completed, but the strange events continued. There have been reports of drinking glasses flying through the air and a piano playing with no one seated in front of it. Dinner guests have seen apparitions and heard strange, unexplained noises.

CITY: St. Louis, Missouri

FIRST REPORTED HAUNTING: 1940s

TYPES OF ACTIVITY: ghost sightings, unexplained noises

SCARY RANKING: 4

ACCESS: The mansion is now a restaurant; they also offer haunted tours.

"At about 3:30 a.m., I was in bed asleep and the springs on the bed started pinging as if someone was under the bed pulling and letting go. I jumped out of bed and [ran] into the hall. I only went back when daylight broke and then only slept on the couch."
—a guest staying at the Lemp Mansion in 1994

patriarch—the male leader of a family

GRAND OPERA HOUSE

You might think of ghosts as terrifying, and the thought of seeing one could send shivers down your spine. But the actors and workers at the Grand Opera House say their spirits are friendly.

The Iowa theater has been the site of hauntings for more than 80 years. Many actors like to practice when the theater is empty, which seems to set the stage for ghostly encounters.

Many of the paranormal events at the Grand are similar to those of other haunted places. Doors open and close with no explanation, and lights turn on and off by themselves. Floorboards creak when no one is walking on them. But it is the voices and ghosts that make the haunting of the Grand famous.

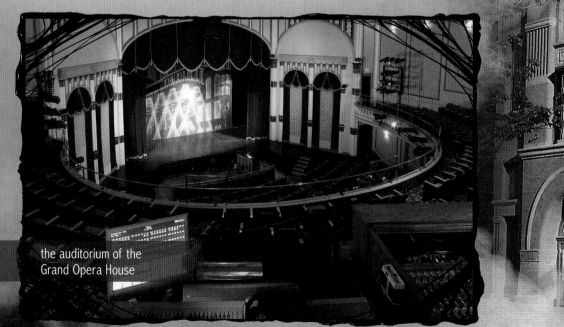

the auditorium of the Grand Opera House

CITY: Dubuque, Iowa

FIRST REPORTED HAUNTING: 1928

TYPES OF ACTIVITY: strange noises, piano music, cold spots

SCARY RANKING: 1

ACCESS: The Grand Opera House was reopened as a theatre with live performances open to the public.

Actors on stage have reported seeing a group of ghosts sitting in the back of the theater. The actors say the ghosts were wearing clothes from long ago. Other actors have reported mysterious voices and singing on stage. In each instance, the theater was empty.

HANNAH HOUSE

CITY: Indianapolis, Indiana

FIRST REPORTED HAUNTING: 1960s

TYPES OF ACTIVITY: unexplained smells coming from an upstairs bedroom, breaking glass in the basement, doors opening on their own, voices in empty rooms

SCARY RANKING: 1

ACCESS: The house is open for tours and events such as wedding receptions.

So much of what makes a haunted house scary can be the building itself. Old Gothic mansions with lots of rooms, basements, and attics leave plenty of space for paranormal guests. One such house, the Hannah House, sits in the heart of Indianapolis. The home was built in 1858, but the first ghosts weren't reported until about 100 years later. People believe two of the spirits are the original owners, wealthy politician Alexander Moore Hannah and his wife, Elizabeth.

Visitors passing by the second floor bedroom have had strange experiences. They reported that the door to the room swung open on its own. Some have smelled rotting flesh coming from within the room. Elizabeth Hannah's baby was delivered in that room, but it wasn't alive. Some people say the room is haunted with death.

the second floor bedroom

The basement of the Hannah House is another hot spot for paranormal activity. Alexander Hannah was reportedly associated with the Underground Railroad. According to legend, tragedy struck one night when a group of slaves seeking freedom stopped at his house. As the slaves slept in the basement, a lamp was accidentally tipped over, which set off a massive blaze. The slaves died. Hannah then buried the slaves' bodies under the basement's dirt floor to cover up the fact that he had been protecting slaves. Visitors and workers have reported crashing, breaking glass, and other odd noises coming from the basement.

One ghost that supposedly haunts the Hannah House is described as "grandfatherly." Some visitors have said the well-dressed man simply disappeared before their eyes. Others, including the granddaughter of a couple living in the home, claimed to have conversations with the ghost. Those who have encountered him describe him as a friendly ghost.

STEPP FAMILY CEMETERY

Like Bachelor's Grove, Stepp Cemetery is a small, out-of-the-way cemetery. No one has been buried there in years. But there is one grave—the grave of a small child—that is said to be haunted.

Legend says the ghost of an old woman sits on a stump next to the child's grave every night. The stump is shaped like a chair, and the ghost keeps watch over the grave.

There are various stories behind the ghost of Stepp Cemetery. The most common story is of a ghostly mother watching over her daughter who is buried in the grave. The daughter was hit by a car and killed, and the mother had the tree cut down to form a permanent seat. Some versions of the story say the woman has put a **curse** on the stump. Anyone who sits on the stump will die exactly one year later.

CITY: Martinsville, Indiana

FIRST REPORTED HAUNTING: 1950s

TYPES OF ACTIVITY: the ghost of a woman near the grave of a young child

SCARY RANKING: 2

ACCESS: The cemetery and surrounding woods are open to the public.

STEPP CEMETERY

ESTABLISHED EARLY 1800s

curse—an evil spell meant to harm someone

ASHMORE ESTATES

CITY: Ashmore, Illinois

FIRST REPORTED HAUNTING: 1970s

TYPES OF ACTIVITY: ghosts and unexplained noises

SCARY RANKING: 1

ACCESS: Ghost tours are available at Ashmore Estates, including overnight stays.

Ashmore Estates was built in 1916 on farmland in Illinois. Originally called the Coles County Poor Farm, it housed people who were poor and needed help. But living conditions at the farm were bad. An estimated 200 people died on the farm. They were buried in a cemetery on the property. The dead included a young girl who was burned in a fire in 1880. Her name was Elva Skinner, and legend says that she haunts Ashmore Estates to this day.

The property was sold in 1959 and was used as a mental hospital until it was closed in 1987. The building was abandoned and became the target of vandals. It was then that the stories of ghosts at Ashmore began to increase. Reports of floating ghosts and unexplained noises at Ashmore spread through the small community. Visitors claimed to hear voices coming from empty rooms. Many people believe that the spirits of those who died on the land are responsible for the hauntings.

"I felt like something was trying to pull me off the floor."
– TV meteorologist Kevin Orpurt describing his stay at the Ashmore Estates

THE GREAT LAKES

LOCATION: The five **Great Lakes** in the Midwest

FIRST REPORTED HAUNTING: 1600s

TYPES OF ACTIVITY: ghost ships sailing years after they sank, apparitions of dead sailors

SCARY RANKING: 1

ACCESS: Most shipwrecks are open to divers for exploration.

The Great Lakes have swallowed more than 6,000 ships and serve as a watery grave for more than 100,000 men. The spirits of the dead are said to live on in the depths of the lakes. But some people believe the ghosts aren't the only things haunting the waters.

The Ghost of "Grandpa"

A dead body on land will quickly **decompose**, but a dead body in icy cold water can be preserved for decades. The SS *Kamloops* sank in 270 feet (82 m) of water off the coast of Michigan in 1927. Divers exploring the wreckage have reported the ghostly corpse of an old sailor trapped within the ship. Nicknamed "grandpa," the ghost is said to be stuck in the engine room of the ship. Divers say that grandpa follows them as they explore the wreckage. Some say it is the spirit of the old man who died when the ship went down. Others say the body simply floats because the divers are stirring up the water.

Great Lakes—a group of five connected freshwater lakes that lie along the border between the United States and Canada; they are Lakes Superior, Michigan, Huron, Erie and Ontario

decompose—to rot or decay

The *Edmund Fitzgerald* was a huge cargo ship that sank in a terrible storm in Lake Superior in 1975. All 29 men on board went down with the ship. One body was found during an exploration dive to the wreckage in 1994, but the other bodies were never recovered. But there have been several sightings of the *Fitzgerald* since 1975. Crews have reported seeing the ship sailing where it was last spotted before it sank. The shattered ship remains 530 feet (162 m) below the surface, so how is it possible that people have seen it gliding on the water?

the wreckage of the
Edmund Fitzgerald

The *Fitzgerald* is just one of hundreds of ghost sightings on the Great Lakes. The first documented ship to sink on the Great Lakes was the *Griffon*, a French supply ship. The *Griffon* was lost on the waters of Lake Michigan in September 1679. For more than 300 years sailors have reported seeing the ghost ship of the *Griffon*. A heavy fog sometimes rolls across the lake. Some visitors have claimed to see the ship emerging from the fog and suddenly vanishing.

HAUNTED PLACES IN THIS BOOK

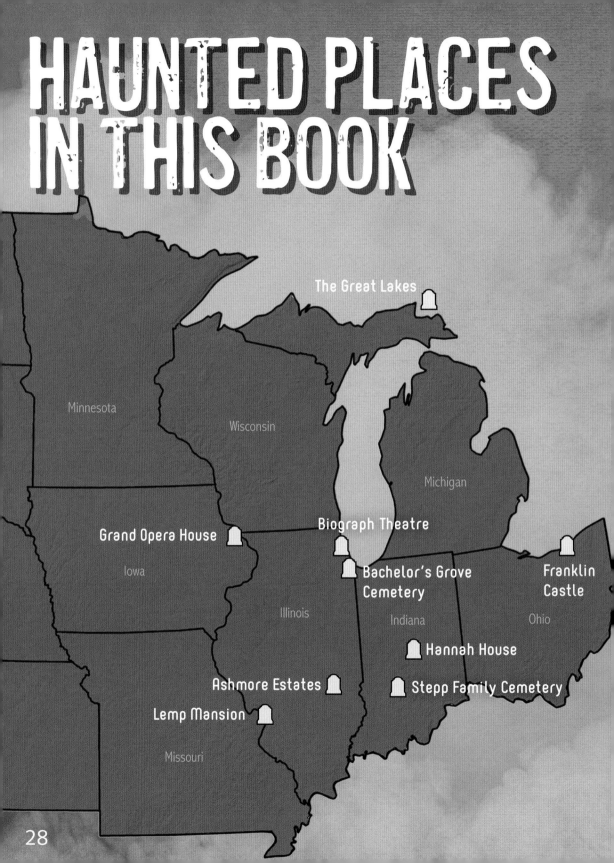

The Great Lakes

Minnesota

Wisconsin

Michigan

Grand Opera House

Biograph Theatre

Iowa

Bachelor's Grove
Cemetery

Franklin
Castle

Illinois

Indiana

Ohio

Hannah House

Ashmore Estates

Stepp Family Cemetery

Lemp Mansion

Missouri

OTHER HAUNTED LOCATIONS OF THE MIDWEST

The Midwest has many other ghoulish places to explore:

- Willard Library in Evansville, Indiana
- Grand Opera House in Oshkosh, Wisconsin
- Sica Hollow State Park in Lake City, South Dakota
- Milton School in Alton, Illinois
- Mason House Inn in Bentonsport, Iowa
- Terrance Inn in Petoskey, Michigan
- The Palmer House Hotel in Sauk Centre, Minnesota
- Liberty Memorial Building in Bismarck, North Dakota
- Octagon House in Fond Du Lac, Wisconsin
- Mission Point Resort in Mackinac Island, Michigan
- Holly Hotel in Holly, Michigan

GLOSSARY

apparition (ap-uh-RISH-uhn)—the visible appearance of a ghost

curse (KURS)—an evil spell meant to harm someone

decompose (dee-kuhm-POHZ)—to rot or decay

Gothic (GOTH-ik)—in the style of art or architecture used in western Europe between the 1100s

Great Lakes (GRAYT LAKES)—a group of five connected freshwater lakes that lie along the border between the United States and Canada; they are Lakes Superior, Michigan, Huron, Erie and Ontario

paranormal (pair-uh-NOR-muhl)—having to do with an unexplained event

patriarch (PAY-tree-ark)—the male leader of a family

Prohibition (pro-hib-BISH-uhn)—a time between 1920 and 1933 when it was illegal to make or sell alcohol in the United States

slavery (SLAY-vur-ee)—the owning of other people; slaves are forced to work without pay

vandalism (VAN-duhl-izhm)—the wrecking of property

READ MORE

Axelrod-Contrada, Joan. *Ghoulish Ghost Stories.*
Scary Stories. Mankato, Minn.: Capstone Press, 2011.

Chandler, Matt. *The World's Most Haunted Places.*
The Ghost Files. Mankato, Minn.: Capstone Press. 2012.

Lunis, Natalie. *Spooky Schools.* Scary Places.
New York: Bearport Publishing, 2013.

INTERNET SITES

FactHound offers a safe, fun way to find Internet sites related to this book. All of the sites on FactHound have been researched by our staff.

Here's all you do:

Visit *www.facthound.com*

Type in this code: 9781476539133

 Check out projects, games and lots more at
www.capstonekids.com

INDEX